Mirror to My Soul

Galaxy Publishing House

This book is dedicated to my parents Brenda H. Allen and in loving memory of my father Phillip R. Allen Sr. who passed away after an agonizing battle with cancer November 8th, 2015. May the light of your existence shine brightly through those you've left behind and your soul rest unto the first resurrection. We love you.

Special thanks to my wife Kendra, my brother Joshua, and my family who have supported me. I love you all dearly.

Table of contents

Mirror to My Soul

I look upon this beautiful one

My hand upon their chest

Secure up in my loving arm

Enjoying my caress

I gently stroke their tiny heads

I love to tickle cheeks

And kiss them on that tiny nose

And rub those little feet

We'll be together always

From young until you're old

More precious than any stone

And oh so dear to hold

Bear witness to this miracle

A blessing to behold

You look at me

I look at you

The mirror to my soul

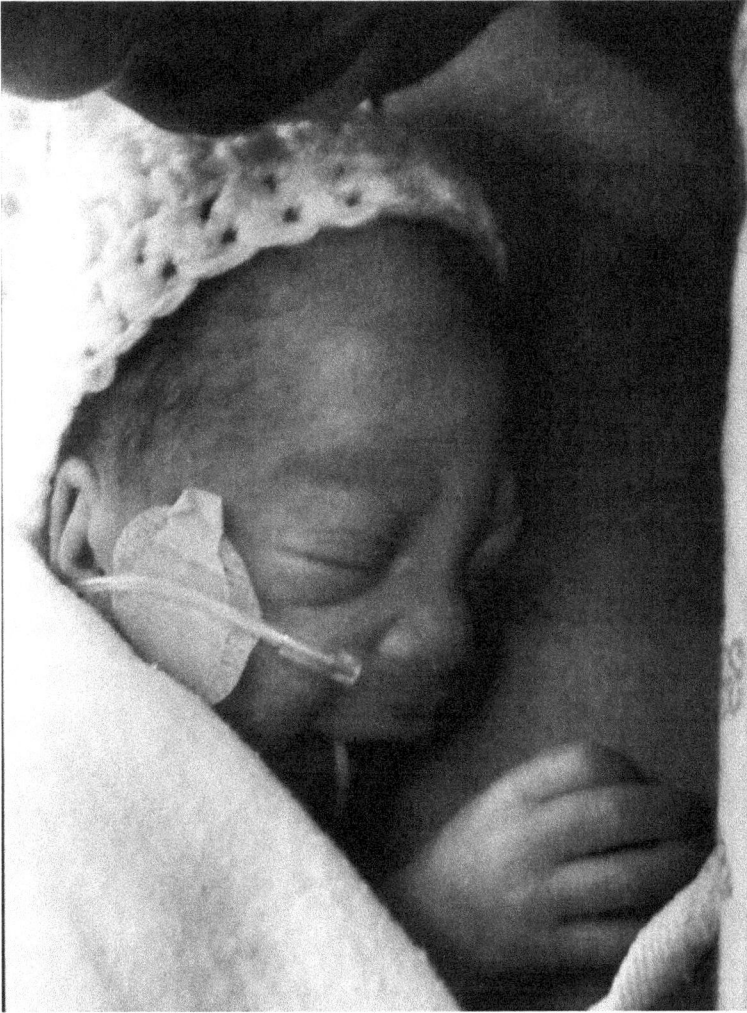

If Birds Could Talk

If birds could talk what would they say

I'd love to talk to a bird someday

I'd ask how it felt to soar through the air

And glide through the heavens without any care

Wouldn't it be great to see what they see

From low lying valleys to great mountain peaks

I'd ask if they really like living in nests

And how do they sleep

Do they get any rest

Can they fly so high that they reach outer space

I know they eat bugs but how do they taste

Are they chewy or salty or sour or sweet

Are they fragrant as flowers or smelly like feet

I heard that birds sing but what songs do they know

Do they like to sing fast or like to sing slow

Just a few questions that I'd like to know

Like during a storm where do all the birds go

Which season is best for them to go play

Which month is their favorite December or May

With all of these questions it seems safe to say

I'll just have to talk with a bird someday

Who are we?

Who am I

Who are you

Who am I to you

Who are you to me

And how do you do

What makes me, me

And what makes you, you

Your future your present

Or the things we've been through

Are you happy or sad

Are you good versus bad

What types of things make you angry and mad

For me I can't stand when people aren't real

I hate fake I hate phony

For me that's a big deal

I like those I can trust

I like those with respect

I like those with ambition without moral neglect

I like those with a purpose

I like those who reflect

I like those who do good unto people they've met

I like those who love YAH

I like those who believe

I like those who don't carry any tricks up their sleeve

But I hate those snakes

You know the ones in the grass

The ones who deceive

The ones who are crass

The ones who do harm to those who walk by

The ones with no truth the first ones to lie

So I'll ask it again

Who are you

Who am I

I know who I am

As for you, you decide

The Devil's an Angel

The devil's an angel that once dwelled in heaven

He served the almighty then picked up and left him

He left his estate to bring chaos to men

He brought famine and pestilence violence and sin

He created religions to make men disagree

And instead of the truth he tells lies when he speaks

He attacks us and tempts us from all different angles

But let's not forget the devil's an angel

He's not a man in a red suit

Nor a bringer of light

He's a master of disguises

A thief in the night

He's not with a pitch fork

Nor lives in hell

No horns on his head

No pointy red tail

He spins deceitful webs

So don't you get tangled

Lest you forget the devil's an angel

He messes your mind and weakens your heart

The taker of souls corruptor of thought

He gets you to do the things you ought not

Defiler of vessels which one day will soon rot

The prince of all darkness

The king of all death

Who people sell out to for fame and for wealth

He and his servants are destined for flames

And though he's an angel

The devil's his name

Words Are Spirit

Words are spirit

They don't even have to rhyme

Some words are like wine

They get better with time

Words can harm

Words can heal

Words can soothe

Words can kill

Words can be simple

Or very complex

Words tell us daily what we are to do next

So choose your words carefully

And watch what you say

Because words can come back

To bite you someday

The Legend of Me

I used to be a baby

Born ten ounces and one pound

And when the doctor delivered me

I didn't make a sound

I opened up my little eyes

And took a look around

I saw my mom I saw my dad

Then they rushed me out

They hooked me up to ventilators

I guess to help me breathe

In the NICU day and night

Three months until I leave

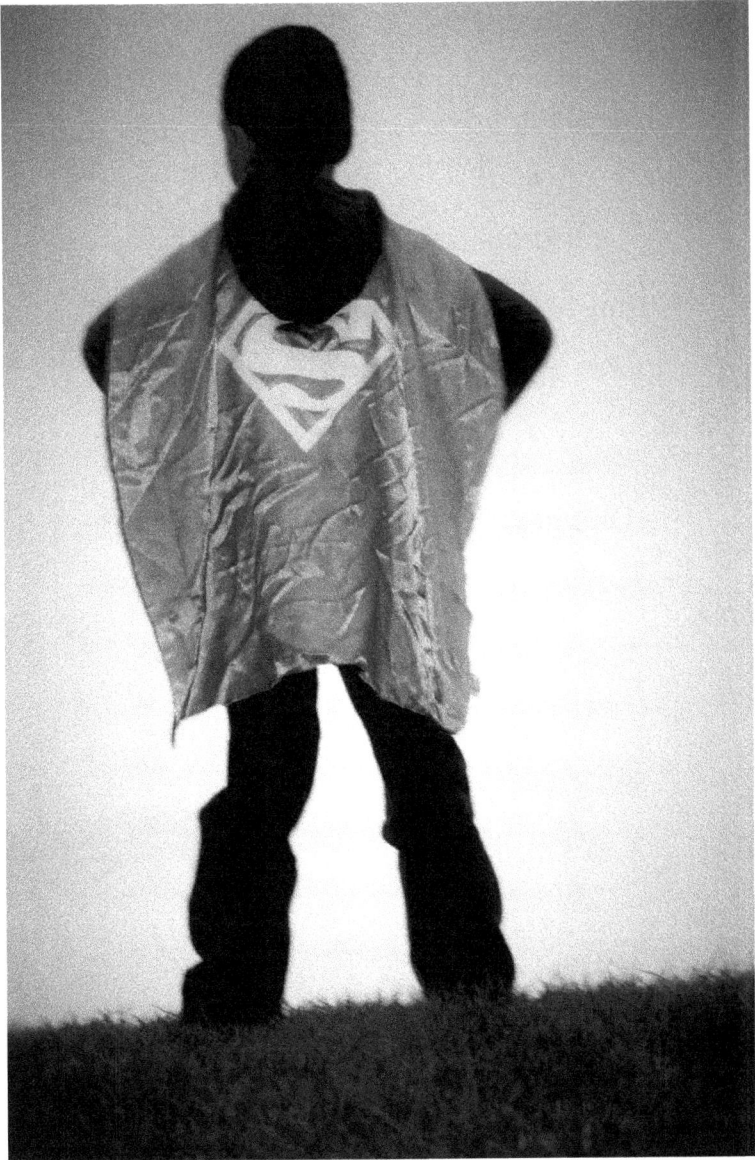

Everyday my folks are here

I know them by their voice

They hold my hand and give me hugs

No choice but to rejoice

One day I'll grow and I'll look back

Though I may forget the pain

I won't forget how far I've come

Yosaiyah is my name

The Reason I Was Born

If I go today please don't cry because it's okay

And if I go tomorrow be not sad have no sorrow

I say this because YAH loves me

He shows me everyday

And when he decides to bring me home

That's where I want to stay

I didn't like it much on Earth

Because of what I saw

With all the sin and suffering

The pain had me in awe

Just thinking about my mother

And all that she goes through

The stress, the pain, daily struggles

So I go through it too

My father was a good man

He was always there at home

Never worried where he was

He taught me right from wrong

I always thought I'd be someone

Someone rich and great

But now I know that's not my path

So I accept my fate

I accept my flaws and all of my mistakes

And I accept the wrongs I've done

I've finally found my faith

So this is for my children

Who will read this when I'm gone

To come to YAH and raise you up

The reason I was born

August 12th (2015)

My 37th anniversary I found out I have cancer

I didn't even ask why because who cares what's the answer

Bottom line is I'm only here for a time

So let me smile and enjoy because every second's my prime

I've lived a long life if you think 60's long

Which I don't, but it is, for my sons I've been strong

I've raised them the best way I know and that's that

Two granddaughters and a grandson who I love that's a fact

I've given plane rides carried them on my back

Laughed with them, talked with them, and I'll miss them so bad

But I know that one day soon I'll see them again

In a place with no violence, no sorrow, no sin

And that is the thought that gets me through my day

It's just me and my wife and together we pray

We pray for forgiveness we pray for shalom

Knowing one day I'll be on my way home

Just know in your hearts that I have no fear

Of death or what's coming because YAH is so near

So remember me singing remember my songs

Remember my rights and let go of my wrongs

Remember my smile remember my laugh

Remember I love you remember your path

And always stay true to yourself and your fam

Let your souls be at peace because finally I am

My Twins and I

I look at both my daughters faces

So proud I have to grin

They radiate with love and warmth

I love my gorgeous twins

I've seen them grow from babies

Though they're only 4 years old

I pray I'm here for many years

To watch their lives unfold

What a blessing two for one is what some people say

For **Ariyah** and **Arieyl** I'm thankful everyday

A picture's worth a thousand words

Some stories go untold

Be kind to your mind and body

Within it lies your soul

Remember that you each are different

Though you look alike I know

Help each other on your paths

Which way you ought to go

Never be jealous of one another

You leave that to the world

And always know even when you're grown

You're daddy's little girls

My Children Are My Crown

I'm a king without a kingdom

A bird without a nest

Hated and despised for the color of my flesh

A slave without chains

Sojourner without rest

Eyes constantly open my whole existence a test

I've asked YAH for forgiveness

For all the wrongs I've done

And what he do

He blessed me with two daughters and a son

I know he smiles upon me

I feel the warm embrace

For that I'll never let the devil shake my family's faith

No matter what earthly things may bring

Into this world of sin

I'm thankful for my lovely wife

Who I can call my friend

See life is but a puff of smoke

That fizzles in the air

And with it all our memories

Our worries and our cares

But never fear salvation comes

I see the heavens part

So from the end a new beginning

We have a brand new start

So till that day we're in the kingdom

I'll live this life awhile

Doing everything within my power

To make my children smile

So though I'm not a king just yet

Won't let that get me down

Because on this Earth I'm truly blessed

My children are my crown

I Am

I am the beginning the Alpha

I am the ending the Omega

I exist of myself

I am eternal

I Am

I am the one who gives life

I am the Creator

I am loving

I am merciful

I am patient

I am Holy

I am righteous

I am without fault

I am the one who created you

I am the one who designed the universe

I am the one who is exalted in Heaven and in the Earth

I AM

I am the one who created time and the one who will end it

I am the truth

I am the light

I am the way

I am the one who has a perfect son in **YAHOSHUA**

I am the one who sent him

I am the one who resurrected him

I am the reason he sits in Heaven awaiting his second time

I am to be loved

I am to be feared

I am to be worshipped

I am the one who makes the Earth tremble in my presence

I am **YAH**

Final Thoughts

A mother's caress is so soft and so gentle

So loving so kind it makes me sentimental

A Father's touch is so perfect so pure

So guiding so firm his love will endure

Together perfection is formed through these two

The combining of souls man woman so true

Sometimes we make life more complex than it is

Through conscience through prayer we should learn how to live

So stay humble be meek and inherit the Earth

Remember the lessons you've learned since your birth

Let no man deceive you through vain words and deceit

And never lay down we can die on our feet

So cherish these words hold them close to your heart

Because your life was planned out before it did start

www.ingramcontent.com/pod-product-compliance
Lightning Source LLC
Chambersburg PA
CBHW070639150426
42811CB00050B/393